As the Den Burns

Poems

Forrest Rapier

TRP: The University Press of SHSU
Huntsville, Texas

Library of Congress Cataloging-in-Publication Data

Names: Rapier, Forrest, author. | Rapier, Forrest. As the den burns. |
Rapier, Forrest. As the den burns.
Title: As the den burns : poems / Forrest Rapier.
Other titles: As the den burns (Compilation)
Description: First edition. | Huntsville : TRP: The University Press of
SHSU, [2022]
Identifiers: LCCN 2022010714 (print) | LCCN 2022010715 (ebook) | ISBN
9781680032819 (paperback) | ISBN 9781680032826 (ebook)
Subjects: LCSH: End of the world--Poetry. | LCGFT: Poetry.
Classification: LCC PS3618.A7258 A9 2022 (print) | LCC PS3618.A7258
(ebook) | DDC 811/.6--dc23/eng/20220311
LC record available at https://lccn.loc.gov/2022010714
LC ebook record available at https://lccn.loc.gov/2022010715

FIRST EDITION

Front cover image licensed via Stock.Adobe.com
Cover design by Bradley A. Ivey

Printed and bound in the United States of America

Published by TRP: The University Press of SHSU
Huntsville, Texas 77341

texasreviewpress.org

Praise for **As the Den Burns**

"Part personal mythology, part fever dream on the Florida coast, *As the Den Burns* introduces a poet with an unmistakable, razor-sharp voice that gets under your skin. Witty, sonic, and place-haunted, these poems have the narrative acuity of Frank Stanford and the fierce imagination of a visual artist steeped in a Bosch-like obsessiveness. Forrest Rapier's poetry is reckless yet accurate, immediate yet historical, cursed yet brimming. The world is on fire in these poems and Rapier is our guide through the rubble, begging us: 'Save what you can.'"

—Nicole Stockburger, author of *Nowhere Beulah*

"*As the Den Burns* thickens and teems with the hardscrabble lives of its Gulf Coast inhabitants. Violence and tenderness, filial piety and escape, disasters and the wild, dangerous beauty of the natural world all appear in Forrest Rapier's stunning heatwave of a debut collection. 'Everything here/is feeding off something else,' he writes, 'Some beasts never evolve.'"

—Leona Sevick, author of *Lion Brothers*

As the Den Burns

Table of Contents

Landscape Umbilical

I.

A thousand miles from a familiar road I feel
low-tide take an inch of beach closer

to the moon's gravity. When I cross
those hazel marshes on the Florida-Georgia line,

I cut my landscape umbilical. Saint Augustine
pier rat born where ospreys yaw at Blackhawk

helicopters. Born where shrimp boats bob
on Saint John's backwater lashing brackish.

The *Jean Ribault* foghorn blares as Swedish
freighters crawl past buoy-poised pelicans,

the gray-feathered elders—wharf guardians
nod silent as the wise men below Gabriel.

II.

Spliff reek piques my ear and every drawl
word I carve makes a bridesmaid blush

wild roses. Ask me about that time I fell
in the Tampa Zoo panther habitat. Ask me

about that time I skated the Apalachicola cemetery
where the witch was burned. Woodpecker

preachers headbang First Corinthians
and exchange promises beneath the wise-ass

Gumtrees. We could be Key West barflies
waiting on floodwaters. We could be watching

firemen stack sandbags—anywhere but here.
Could be anyone. Who rises and is risen?

From the cavern tomb, Dawn
buttons his white suit for Easter.

I.

"…the banished youth throwing his discus into the sea the long swim into exile…"
The Battlefield Where The Moon Says I Love You

One Thousand Tongues

I.

Static-throated Florida growler, heat
      lightning trapped behind his iris—

he broadcasted my birth
        —a storm worth
watching—Neptune Beach

      scratched-out by hurricanes
like a pocket-knife on a school desk.

II.

I'm the brainchild of a lifeboat and a flare-gun
        —single-shot dynamo corkscrewing
against a sky jacket of torn tweed.

III.

Noon flares jukebox mosquito music
      on his whitewashed front porch.

      Before knocking on Radio Pop's door,
wild light shreds a whorl of lost feather.

IV.

      Radio Pop, everything is biblical—
the hundred-year-old foursquare house
      under perpetual repair, a gopherwood

ark built to save a few strays, the sun's infinite
      redaction. Your arguments with God,

saying things like *I'll tell you how dark
      it gets* and *you have to be stealth*—

a slipknot of cicada husks split-open and shed
      beneath the table saw buzz. Spitting image,

blue drums rise—one thousand tongues
      crash on the mouth of a cove.

Summer's jar of drowned flies,
      with a broken wing, the raven sings of land.

Millennia of Heck

All he has in this world: Panhandle twang,
    untuned Tallahassee Salvation

        Army Fender Stratocasters, hurricane
            strays and wild chickens for brains.

        Furious blazes shock his palms
holy-broken—his feet remember

        lightning turning dunes
into God's blown glass. In class,

riptide-waisted blondes misunderstood
        his problematic accent like a chalkboard

            gibbering algebra—his buckshot language
                follows a blueprint of dead stars.

        Bloodshot retina, dishwater moptop,
restless warbling circling brick smokestacks

        —he exists beneath Georgian traintracks
where azaleas boom utopic in a hogweed haven.

        Once, he was the ark's dove
        heckling every animal with a branch
        out both sides of his mouth—whatever
            they say traces scars

        like gossip behind his back.

Fathermark

I.

Unmedicated visionary,
full-time armchair operator—
he could turn a truckbed of scrap lumber

to a hen house squared-up enough no fox
could slide. Lucky roosters peck cornmeal
grain-by-grain off the earth—call it God's stopwatch.

II.

Through my voicemail phone-static,
Mark jabbers his bus station Radio Shack
logic as bankrupt-outdated-short-circuit

mallrats skitter listless, shelling
their collective family peanut-memory
against spotlessly-flawed marble floors.

III.

Alabama River reeds hum
his floodname after a Gulf hurricane
watermarks all the downtown brick

buildings. For years, I was blindsided
by County jail phone calls, splotchy postcards
signed *love*—the word was a phantom

licking stamps in the dark.

Radio Pop

I.

After lifeguards fried his chest with a defibrillator,
my father started picking-up Christian radio
     stations with his brain.

His hippie beach-lingo and surfboards
were replaced by invisible blondes
     swinging flaming swords.

Mark became Radio Pop and recorded
my fat legs whirling tricycle pedals
     —it was a tornado he was chasing.

II.

Soon, Neptune Beach dunes will erode
like equations erased off a chalkboard
     by hurricane waves. My mouth's

a rubber band aimed at a juice box.
Underneath my school desk
     I'm scratching my pocket-knife

to cut Jessica D's initials
inside a crooked-wooden heart.
     Later that night at baseball,

my father handed me some cookies
through the outfield chain link fence.
     When I looked back at the diamond,

he was gone. A boy named Christian
bit the head off my gingerbread man
     and I knocked his tooth loose in the dugout.

III.

My father circles constantly,
points to his palms and swears
　　　he can see the stigmata.

On the plateau, Elijah's mother
told me *to try and touch anything Christlike
　　　is to abandon faith*.

Chiaroscuro

Below the table salt galaxy of spilled life,
    Lake and I watch heat lightning mime
        hummingbird tongues as warm

rain scars the azaleas. Flashing branches split
    the sky in-half as fat squirrels argue
        who bit the last crabapple

        in the chicken-scratch driveway gravel.
    Leo struts his snakeskin boots
out on the deck, purrs the blowtorch

        blue over a bowl of shatter—oil
bubbles tulips in the honeycomb chamber.
Lake coughs a wildfire backdraft glass hive.

        If there's no church in the wild, why do alleyway
    tigers yowl a stray prayer? *Tallahassee* is an Apalachee
word meaning *abandoned fields*. Leo empties

a Winchester box of shotgun shells and we burn
    half-the-yard with an orange juice jug
        filled with Gulf gasoline.

Leo stomps on little fires like peanuts husks
    stamped on steakhouse floorboards.
        Laughing at him, Lake trips an anthill

as oaks ash Spanish moss across dark grass.
    He rises through a cathouse door of dead stars.
        I pour hot wax on the moon's lower back.

        Jade surf lashes Jupiter skiffs—I know the handcuff
pinch behind my back, the boxcar vibrato on midnight
camellias, the forgotten shipwreck's watermark on hidden shoals.

Burial

Habitually kneeling afore an estranged creator's
    stained windows, the holy son
lived in his Mother's patient stomach.

    Prayers blessed her chest, along with
priests' bony hands and the frail odd
    women tonguing psalms—

nothing saved him. To be born,
    wrapped in a swathe of wrath
and carried away—buried immediately.

    My faith lays in the dirt with that child.
Boy, water a field of apology so your Mother
    may sow. I would have taken his place,

exchanged my life of revenant fingernails
    and crossroads—light hammers my palms.
Painters smack canvas backdrops black,

pull God from the shade. How do they do it?
    How do I carry this fatherbeast in my chest?

Disturbed Mud

I.

Reckless drums pound buckskin beats
inside the headstrong horseman
riding under shadow of no moon.
Embers steady, then flare like blue
cornfields untended for a season.
Two decades of snow on his face and he still doubts

the springtime predictions written-in-corollas
on the firstborn foal's bloody forehead.

II.

This summer, he has hacked every outskirt azalea bush
and whispered gratitude to the fog obscuring his scent.

He rows a loaded boat of white azalea upstream,
whorls old songs from his young lungs and pulls

the pine oars shoreward. He hauls the woven wreath
to Grandfather Pond where roe fawns graze on sweetgrass.

III.

He will grow to know an ambush by the disturbed mud,
a trail of saw palms beat-back by dull hand-axes.

Nude rivals crouch behind that mossy log.
He traced their footprints, obvious like foxfur
pressed in yesterday's sleet.

Hush—they will cut off our hair
if we fall asleep.

Rowing Out of a Riptide

Whiskey-blurred Panhandle mutterer
    rowing a canoe over eelgrass,
toothpicking his Lake City
        lowland youth
like wild blackberries,
                he's strumming trail myths
from memory, hammering
                    porch floorboards up a key,
patching drywall or driving nails
                        half-an-inch into the lonely
                ghost of some lost saint
stuck as a fly on a honeytrap windowpane;
            you know he's working Thomas
Street doubt-houses poorer than a churchmouse
        shelling peas in an echo bucket,
fixing to fix-up more unending babble.

While straw-thin litterboys collected ditch
bottles to cash-in for mint-chocolate-chip
    slide nickels on a dimestore countertop,

        my first conscious fleck happened
    afloat a milk jug raft
drifting past the Gulf sandbar.

    My fathermyth swam his flipper palms
against the axis—riptides riffed
    my blue existence into note.

    Gravity, the power of love—it's all one
tune the godchild's whistling on Time's bridge.

Hovering Gatekeepers, the rambling bookworms
    keep scrolling through your bright disasters.

Detention

The windshield pollen layer was thick as bean
dip when June struck jasmine and honeydew

shine through the arrow-slit pane of glass
in the classroom door—there's the asthmatic

janitor puffing his albuterol
inhaler, forgetting to erase

whatever chalkboard arithmetic
kept me stumped for months like an archer

in detention trying to knock poetic
rhythms on a desktop. I counted

leopard spots in the overhead lights
made by dead moths and time's movement

in Roman numerals; how would I know
my hands from every other damned thing?

Missing perfect surf because I cheated
on the Earth-Space science exam

because the librarian's daughter
wanted to burn Sour Diesel off Oak

Street because we wanted to kiss and blend
brains because we both had eyes like chill ponds

because ten thousand years ago people
mutated because of Earth-Space science.

After Matthew

I.

Hurricane Matthew shredded rose gardens
     to mottled petals and torn thorns, split
       century-old Spanish Oaks from raw earth

like tidepool toys the sudden crash swallows.
  Mercury balanced on Chloris' breath

     in the swollen, smoky Cummer Gardens
summer daze of Florida haze,
carried-over the Saint John's River
by tropic zephyrs and purp clouds.

The storm left a mess of strays
hounding our screen doors, scared
and scarred, they scratched for feed.

Who could blame them for begging
    for whatever we had that they didn't?

II.

Dogs clawing at the porch door like the time
I carved my name beneath the church pews.
All of us just trying to let the master know
where we were and what we wanted.

My fathermark sidemouths sunflower
seeds on his Lil' Champ gander,
gathers ion threads that lets us know
where everybody we love is
and what they're trying to say. Say
I'm trying to be someone better
than the place where they learned
how not to die, how to ride out hard rain.

Wish I understood half-of-what he said.
Have to listen to the way they say it.

III.

He'd strum his ferryboat shoreward, talk
cigarette-static through his vocal chords
like he were finger-picking a cigar
box guitar for the jazz crowd.
His voice was a sharp set of twang
strings, tuned like Alabama River
reeds poking upstream as daybreak
horizons rise red-eyed—tired
and hungover, my fathermark
has that marsh iris like a heron's beak
threading stitches in the pawpaw.
He'd take me up on the pier,
weigh me on the fish scale
right there, for the world to see.

IV.

In the schoolroom slide-projector half-dark,
acne-scarred fools tried to lift Danyelle's skirt
when she lit late through History's door
like August hibiscus or Caravaggio's red
shawls painted around the bone-thin
shoulders of insane saints. Luke muttered
curse words loud-soft behind her ear, twisted
her ombre hair around the chewed-end
of his blunt No. 2 and snapped his pencil
in-half. Was Jesus the first omniscient
grub born fatherless in a hut under a straw
roof? Danyelle, don't spark the hammer
beneath your jaw. Ward—her last name
means guard. Keep roaring in that den.

Lackawanna Crib

I.

Mark's tweaked skull cracks
faster than an absinthe-riddled painter
rolling facedown on a blank canvas.

He knows Lackawanna is a bruise
under his eye—a strange forest where
boar hunters toss sow reek on bark.

II.

Millennia-old stalactites shoulder
the world's heft. Beneath the Hart Bridge,
Mark shoots a school of silverfish

through his forearm rip
current veins and endless breezes
urchin through his sharpened heart.

III.

Last week's spitbottle bobs in Westside
gutter ponds where ankle-deep kids reel

meaningless catfish. They say *lord*
flopping blood in the gold-lit grass.

Everybody walking out of that water
comes homes slick as the day they were born.

Panhandle ocelots purr
sweet as church carnival caramel corn.

Cypress razors fan lush—Ruth's knockout
roses pink back from the dead

sudden as dew, the fishscale glint through
cooler ice when you lift the lid to see.

IV.

Born upside-down under a cow tooth moon
in Cathedral Caverns, his translucent wings pop
    open behind his back. My fathermyth, the lost
pilot skittering batty unto a savage horizon.

Atlantic Baptism

Hook pierced in his bottlenose, tangerine
sun-tanned barracuda boy
     articulating the magnolia
        lavish Peninsula—invasive
constrictors weave ten feet of snakeskin
and cut muscle through kudzu
     forests, camouflaged by green hell.

     Chest-pump fueling fires
bluer than a whale's eye, he led sublime
angelfish schools to an offshore reef, guided
lost ships homeward without lighthouses
        poised on a cliff's edge—he is rising
out of his Atlantic baptism
like a bookworm
     when the library intercom announces
final checkouts and fifteen minutes.

He wore a denim jacket
     bluer than a whale's eye, wriggled electric
eels through wayward Neptune's riptide beard.
Ancient mangrove root protector,
Everglades mosquito
     orchestra conductor,
you may find him sweating bullets
       at Lake Okeechobee's slick edge
fishing two poles at dock's end, waiting for dusk
     like a friend—you never have to speak,
       you know exactly what they think.

The Book of Ruth

I.

    She's squinting beyond the aluminum
graph paper-thin barrier, wearing her canary
    yellow sweater in the middle of July.

Her screen door hinges speak creak
    futures of teak forests talking bark
tongues—even screws have voices.

II.

    Ruth's face runs deeper than every waterway
winding the panhandle—her hallway
    bookshelves stand tall as cornfield stalks.

Her lionfish hands spine veins, weightless
    as a letter. The dining room's shaded by lace
drapes and banana leaves. Through the widow's

    window, old shoes hang—two
ravens strung over phone pole wires.

III.

Ruth's lungs hum Georgia summers cracking
    skies like milk teeth or piggy banks

smashed by a baseball bat. Penny thunderheads
    rumble while I wolfwhistle at the scent of her
frying johnny cakes in bacon fat.

    Doubt-wild chickens chase hen feathers
across Thomas and Edison Street.

What good is a shoebox of photographs
    to a woman who can barely measure flour by eye?

IV.

Mark is a ship sealed-in glass—I'm his spitting
image tiptoeing circus tightropes blindfolded.

Neptune Beach

Raised out of eroded dunes and floodwater
markers. Raised out of tightened-up nets

where shrimp boats ebb near the dock's
edge, where mud-wise pelicans weave

waves together with the eastern light.
Out of sawgrass slick, salt lick for the swamp

buck wandering into the pink. Raised
out of Ophelia's eyewall, Rita's surge

rushing over the Oak Street sandbags.
Raised out of Tropical Storm Tammy

knocking powerlines down and dragging
surfers beneath her wicked rip. Out of

Wilma lifting an entire Lake City
pasture, pouring buckets by the second.

Raised out of low tide mussel beds mouthing
up at the Apalachicola lighthouse—out of mud

slop on Saint George Island and sun-bleached
driftwood mangled on Alligator Point.

Out of Neptune Beach magnolia gravel crunch
beneath Chevrolet wheel-wells, beneath Spanish

moss dripping from a jet-black fish-eye-sky.
Out where the wordless guardians rearrange us

piece-by-piece like jigsaw nirvana. Transfixed
by the painted horses grazing on Cumberland Island

fescue, I rose out of the water tower
to keep watch over my minuscule coastal town

because no one else would promise they'd stay
up for all that mess and God knows what after.

From Jupiter

> Off Florida's East coast, two shirtless boys
> thump barefoot down a dock with a bait
bucket and a hundred dollars worth of gas.

> Whitewater hit the slip—Perry
> gunned after a school of Mahi Mahi
Austin spotted on his fish radar.

Nobody on the pier looked twice
when they hauled-off into a storm
the Coast Guard dubbed *typical*

> *South Florida*—heavy rain, thunder.
Nine days after they left Jupiter,
> > the Coast Guard found a boat

capsized eighty miles offshore
> —one orange jacket tethered to a lifeline.
> > No one can predict a rogue wave.

> Perry's mother said,
> "These children are surrounded by water
from the moment they're born."

Did they bob near the wreckage?
Survive the first night's storm, float
> in inky infinity like corks on a wine sea?

Five thousand miles across the world,
> Hawaiian flower pistils pink
> > alight Kilauea cooled magma.

A flare shot from a shuteye
> ocean—we hope you see us.
> > We're right here.

Curse

Your face unfastens, a loose button
on a blouse in a hot church.
Your mouth curves into a shovel head.

Stones fall upon your tongue. Blood
on a quail feather. Dirt smears
across your lips. Open your mouth—

Razorblades. A raven shot
through the back of its beak.
Ice poured onto grass. Over there,

your house on top of the hill.
It is burning. Your dog runs
through the doorway.

Her fur is on fire. Your
husband opens his mouth
in the dark. A cocoon.

A field of cicada husks.
A field of cotton ablaze.
A drawer of dull knives.

A crown of barbed wire.
Somebody's going to write
your name, sweetheart.

Your name here,
three times. Then X,
after X, after X.

A necklace of pulled
teeth. A field of corn gone
bone. No more honey.

II.

"I see you young blades living dangerously,"
The Odyssey

Panther

I.

The river makes people go crazy—he's from a hurricane
    alley where weather comes home angry-drunk,

crushes the popsicle stick fishing pier
    like it's a spinal-cord built for the science fair.

II.

    When he brought the glued-wreckage to class,
six-hundred strange teeth

    laughed behind school desks, then he misspelled
'nationalism' in the gymnasium bee.

    The asphalt canopy where he's from flaunts
streetfruit names—Orange, Lemon, Cherry.

    Every summer, it's one after another:
Glen took one-in-the-chest at Seawalk Pavilion.

Danyelle shot her neck in a Queen
    bed near Egret's Bluff.

Now they paint chameleon scales with light
    over every Panhandle shade garden.

III.

    Haloed-zero friends of his tongue nectar with alien
hummingbirds on Neptune's undiscovered beach—they fly

    V-flocks over frozen oceans. Once,
he was the last panther in the Everglades

    screaming through a cyclone's rain.

Primordial Shriek

I.

Stick lightning rods in Neptune dunes
like a leatherback burying itself
on this beach where I keep watch.

Litterbug tourists and know-it-all snowbirds
erase the orange stratos solace horizons
piece-by-piece—they toss screw-top

bottlecaps and cigarette ends into tidepools
where sandpipers and dead-eyed gulls waver.
Summers: thunder shreds the saltwater

musk atmosphere into unsolvable
jigsaws. Irreparable angel wings fall
near a shattered tiger eye—few

hatchlings survive the long crawl
across this haywire shoreline.

Sunset-headed toddlers
wobble their tricycle handlebars
as stained-hoodie sidewalk parents
shout *yes* and *no* into neurosis-speakerphones.

II.

Every neighbor's nosing forward
like a tweaked greyhound
sprinting after a false-rabbit:
this is how a country flames out.

Frizzy-bun spider-eyeliner
errant-wanderers blitz past
the grocery stock-boys opening
diaper boxes with a razor.

State Park firefighters doze in watchtowers
as pyromaniac teenage campers
blowtorch cardboard beer boxes in a drought.

Wander off toward your nearest creek.
Given the right light, you may find
a neolithic spearpoint

to be recovered from a muddled
eon—welcome to your ancient life.

Workbench Dust

My fathermark shouts at the cathedrals
shielding Earth—he's a tempest-templed,
cock-eyed weathervane speaking

creeks of sawteeth, passing down a broken
brain in a word-cursed bottle—I'm a bubble
dome sapling in a lumber scent neighborhood

of empty new rooms. No divorces, only doorways.
You cannot divide by zero. Tweaked seagulls
beak pearl fish from the lightless sea.

Mark's loose as a ditch tire—his table saw
logic roars like lion jaws

lording savanna ballads for the zebras
dozing under daybreak acacias.

Who spills uncaged word surf, speaks-in-currents
like mazes only the seaturtles could navigate?

Study the chalk dust
blown across a carpenter's workbench:
it could be first frost icing dead grass.

Save your bag boy cash and unfold
crinkled dollars on the drugstore counter.

Pop a can of Barbasol as Ichetucknee
River pressure cracks a freediver's lamp.

Face-to-face with a plastic razor
poised afore his spitting image;
how fast will the sun redact us?

Wolf Hour

Outside, those first shy blips of wolf hour
rain drop like coins on a blue velvet guitar
case tipped-open in Railroad Square.

The way Lake twists his neck:
headless, Nike of Samothrace
shipwrecked against television battle-blur.

Standing at the sink's bowl, the faucet peters
thin as Fahrenheit graduation marks—dust
lifts off the bent Venetian blinds.

The bubble-screen dresses Lake
in a blur-colored houndstooth blazer.
After midnight talk show hosts hock

false laughter, I flip Spirit
cigarette ends off the deck edge.
Pretend there's fish swimming

in the crabgrass where every shred of pine
straw sharpens as the moon cuts snow
across her mirror of blackgrass.

Tallahassee Nightwatch

A few doors down, Wiley's lemons rot
beneath his stilted porch and the Shelby
blinks through his garage window.

I'm outside with all my sleepless animals,
waiting for the sky to decide weather or not,
listening to barred owls root for our college yards.

Right out of sawgrass, Georgia thunderheads
sketch a horse iris out of Florida heat lightning.
Every dot pulses like the veins on a foal's eyelid.

Last night, we kept vigil through the rain-band parade
like Spanish mustangs were surging through high tide
underneath a fish hook eclipse—I got a nosebleed.

Cross-street, Leo's lampshade clicks-on
illuminating the cherry-red Fender Stratocaster
humming chords into a mounted four-point

buck's perky ears. My neck gets wet
from a few fat drops. I'm thinking about Bailey
reaching for her eyeglasses in the Ozark half-dark.

Leo's grinning through his blinds—chain-smoking
insomniac. My rooftop rooster weathervane
tracks the wind-creak with metal talons.

I'm a hyacinth-throated
peacock plucking a cedar guitar,
snapping strings at dawn.

Vision of the Cliff Divers

Go to Kingpin's blacklight den
    for your Tallahassee research
        chemical rite-of-passage.
    Watch the witch hours ash
Parliament after Parliament
    until whirligig starlings pink the chirp
        dawn, then Rite of Spring
    then scratch a poem. Wrozynski
commented, "spell things correctly"
    and "why do we care?" Consider this
        my Panhandle comeback
    sprinting through a wildfire treeline
like Roan horses let loose. Rival tribes
    burn the treeline—each day
        I rise alive with language-knowledge
    flying where no one may follow.
My brain is a caged hawk.
    Spearmen squat in morning mud and speak:
        there's ash on the cornflowers and *the bear
    god is late*—they worry about flags
and messengers being misinterpreted.
    Rivals—nothing is growing
        because our discordant families
    have abandoned the mud ritual.
We stay leaning backwards always like shade
    grass in summer squash wind, drifting
        downriver in the rowboat where I fish
    good days from memory's blue hole.
Wavy signals rise from the cedar fire: lifeless
    coral, turquoise necklaces smashed against
        stone, then countless rain. Nameless Vanity,
    my contusion full of ageless angels is poised.
Mirror Lake Seer, I foretold the know-nothing
    vanguards who flew off the cliff
        edges to scream bloody prayer for hours;
    nobody healed them. We waited like dogs
in the unmoving evening when the wind is Grandfather
    still. Leaning back from the watchfire, I smoke
        creek weed and wait for the buried pig

to be dug out from the earth. Shoo, I'm Colt
Never To Be Broken—the Creator is perfect light,
    always sharing corn and the nail goes in clean,
        then the edge of the world burns off
like frayed thread from a dress.

Appaloosa Rider Unchained

Your horses ride today to set you free.
No longer shall your voices be contained,
or chained to the watchman's land without a key.
Here, blades and bows—weapons keep the peace,
yet who provides shelter beyond the walls of rain?
Your friend will yell your name, then set you free.
Ignite the fires. The song becomes the key.
Unlock yourselves from umber cages, terrains
of soot no longer bind you. Never lose this key.
Longboats await offshore. Together we
ford rivers of golden grain. Steady the reins
of your horses. Let them break away. Let them be
unafraid. When darkness falls we ride across the plains.
Unbury your family plainsongs from the grave deep
inside your throat. Sing out the missing key.
Reclaim your ancient speech from amber plains. See
beaches aflame. History ashen again.
Our friends will yell our names. They set us free.
If your horse breaks away, let them be.

Everything Here

is feeding off something else. Smoke
feeds the vice, vices feed the river
which feeds shrimp to fish which feed us
and we feed the cycle—the devour
cycle. Florida is a constant state of flux.
Animal Control officers net a bullgator
hissing in a Ponte Vedra sand trap.
Some beasts never evolve.

When its stomach lining is cut-open,
a woman's missing arm is found.
Powerlines quaver the frenetic voices
of seatown wives to midnight phonebooths
keeping watch at the wharves—humpback
whales rough barnacles off their gigantic
chins with freighter-underbellies
they use as razors. Here, yard-sharpened

aloe vera leaves thrive with lotion veins
near the Saint John's inlet where ferryboat
foghorns howl tadpole legs out of thin air.
Everything here is feeding off something.
Feeding off a vice or a lie. Gadflies and ticks
drink bloodsweat off a cow's neck sweat
while sun-spotted lostboys hock dried rattlesnake
skins for loose change thrown out a car window.

Flammable youths orchestrate the parking lot
smoke rings before school doors unleash a June
exodus like a transatlantic cicada migration.
Obstenarian doctors pull an underweight
miracle into the breath-shocked newborn
world—his empty-handed father stands
near bottle-necked Peach Soda delivery trucks
in a black-and-white photograph.

I've waited for years to hear a panther
yowl like hell in the hidden castilleja.

Fatherbeast

I.

Californian landslides level
hundred-year old ponderosa pines,
Key Largo devil rays slice jade waves
near sunken mangrove forests, floating fruit
abandons the native shoreline for foreign
spits of rock where ospreys nest—my father
spent years of his life paddling a longboard
through endless tubular curling barrels
off the coast of Baja Mexico while
I cut anthill-bumps under my neck
and brushed my crooked yard of teeth.

II.

Now, he fills my brainmail with his voicebox;
how many years did he spend quietly
going back on his word? Sobriety
isn't an appointment you call and reschedule.
Facedown on Neptune Beach white-sand, I watch
red-shoulder toddlers in water-wings chase
rat-tail haircuts through tidepools.
Earlier, in the dawn-lit 24-hour casino,
two barflies split cigarettes and a
plastic cup of Chardonnay—the bald
bartender skeeved me out like a cue ball
jumped the table and found a job.
Curious gulls waddle toward my newspaper
as if the *Wall Street Journal*'s a hunk of bread
worth fighting for—armored cops shrug
on a cover story. If a gun fires in Florida,
does anybody hear it?

III.

All these fringe coastal areas littered
with lightning-struck lostboys—misguided
violet-eyed suicidal firearms riding bicycles
and raising hell as gnats corkscrew a waterfall.
Paramedics lift a body, free of God
like strays nursed by a wolfmother.

IV.

Backlit invisible: do clouds feel
the bolt go from murmur to curse?
Where we're from, cicadas buck and dance
a rotunda-harmonica slew of slay thyself.
Go missing in Florida, die and get found.

Beneath the Lemon Tree

Jamming Fender Jaguars in a cinderblock
garage on Pepperhill Court—Victor's black

Labrador barked the cue ball moonrock off
the world's shredded felt tabletop. Weekends:

fatback grease solidified in a skillet crater
until I'd scour it onto the elephant ears

listening outside—Doak Campbell Stadium
yowled for blazing spear throwdowns, touchdowns.

In the overdosing sundowns, we'd scream for dead head
nobodies, chug Drop D chords on cherrywood axes.

We'd lollygag on bottom-shelf Winstons—I think
our first band name was Oatmeal Mush. The Shark

House in Tallahassee was a moshpit in a hotbox
where gumdrop spice-punks tongued paper-thin

gasoline-tasty smiley-face strips. One guy's
septum ripped-out when Chewbacca Yawp

dropped into breakdown—Stratocasters thrashed
like scalding pots in a witch's vineyard. Day after a show,

I'd drive to get a dozen honey-butter-chicken-biscuits.
Matthew'd snore like a chainsaw splitting a pin oak

until Falcons kickoff—my brainpan was on low-heat
all day like a pot of spaghetti sauce. Enjoy this little

rainwater catch-barrel I've been milling near all day,
leg propped on the porch banister, nursing

a swollen kneecap with an Igloo ice pack—frost
dripping as the shadow dog humbles over to lick.

Yawping Gargoyles

Protect the Panther license plates and Jurassic period
mega-Gators hissing at golfers—unburied
conquistador wanderers search for limestone
slabs where their name is written: Florida's
where melanoma-riddled mechanics
clean a year of grease from a battleship
engine with an old bandana. Rusty thaws flounder,
throws a fish fry for everyone on their last-leg

in Mayport Village. I was a little dot
inside my mother's body when she was diving
with the parrotfish darting from the barracuda.
Two firefighters go missing for two weeks and their boat's
never found. If I spent the peak of my monthly focus
searching through a smoking room, looking for a body
the fire wanted, I'd be out on open water every weekend
the chop was low. Florida Easter smells like jasmine

wrapped fenceposts where lizards wrestle lizards.
Tallahassee: church spire shadows on asphalt
where potbelly police can't outrun a skateboard.
Yesteryear soda-shop graffiti fades on a cinderblock
pourhouse where wing-tipped rumrunners shoulder
every wayward idiot wasting his check on keg dregs.
Look above the fluted pillars: yawping gargoyles
guard a most unholy gate—they'll let anybody in.

How much hectic weight can you shoulder?
Gangly groups in dog hair sweaters swap
tubes of lilac lipstick. Everybody here
becomes wax paper on a butcher's scale;
a blood-red flank to be weighed and wrapped.
New Year's Day: putting on my wetsuit like a walrus
hulking into a tent. Undercurrent tore the leash off
my ankle—surfboard flew like Voyager beyond Neptune.

Godchild

I.

Imagine God's a kid splashing water
      over a tub lip, pulling zebras
         from the suds. He's hiding

yawning lions under a Mr. Bubbles savanna.
     Yesterday, he tore out dawn's braid.
        Haloed chubby baby boy

       waddling to lay on hay
   and weave a twisted fantasy:
dying while Mary watches.

II.

Fish swagger beneath frozen
streams like directionless people
fording memory-headwaters

to milk the cream inside holy cows.
Most of this world carries water buckets
from a well, gathers straw for the night fire.

He'd groggy-wake to pancakes
stacked five-high—honey and hot syrup
slick a smackers-faded scar.

He overturned her guts, kicked her in utero;
the world, the womb—it's all a warm bath
her son never survives.

III.

Jane's wet denim eyes sag like a shawl
        shaded on the Virgin's shoulders.
            When's Mary going to start

frying chicken thighs? Yesterday,
        the ordinary pantheon of stars
            popped out like hot grease.

III.

"we shook hands then we stood there her shadow high against his shadow one shadow"
The Sound and the Fury

To a Spotted Horse in Middleburg

Faded dunes shook loose from the Sea
oats guarding Neptune Beach—gone.

Gone are the spray-painted sidelines where
bombshell cheerleaders chanted *Go* for two

hours and the Gatorade cooler froze. My center's
breath blew into the neutral zone like frost

threads immobilizing the community garden.
Blackhawk helicopters circle beneath meteor

showers in the swamp dark—long gone
are those mottled apples I fed

to the spotted horse in Middleburg. Gone:
fried chicken shacks greasing birds in honey

pepper sauce and brewing tea sweet enough
to hurt your teeth. Cleat-digs along hash marks,

helmet smacks echoing inside my brainpain
like a colony of bats—my Neolithic skull

hurt beautifully like a French cavern
painted with thumb-mammoths in my own

blood. Eventually, summer tomatoes will
ripen out of flowerboxes as the July skies

crack electric blue with gunpowder dusk.
Florida horizons the peach juice to sunburst

above the ballpark. Gone. Waited all my life for Peace
to fall on Earth with Mercy—two concussed angels

wandering bleary-eyed through storm-soaked pastures.
They plunge their all-seeing hands into rank dirt and laugh.

If they were here, would we recognize these inglorious
guardians? Would we ignore their inexplicable reek?

Jesus, I'm sure they'd be babbling, too.
Smelling like the whole farm. Gone.

Firewheel

for Jenniver

She will never be a legendary ghost
ship haunting the Alaska horizon,
or mythic grasslands where Bonnaroo

wanderers search for vegan wraps and the Who
Stage. By pure will, by the skin of her teeth,
she survived cancer twice while I was laying

backwards in Tennesseean fields listening to
Dead & Company jam. Her battlefield lungs
torn-to-rubble by Big Tobacco,

workplace asbestos and blitzkrieg chemotherapy.
I was her peacemaker with sandy legs,
trying to splash-wash the beach brine

from my feet with one ankle in the sink
while she slept through re-runs of Card Sharks
beneath her painting of blackbirds.

Costume pearls clamored out of a wood box I painted
at Camp Immokalee. The word is much like the land:
translated from Calusa to Seminole to asphalt

to sheet metal billboard to mean *my home*.
Florida: Land of Imprisoned Orca, brackish
haven where manatees breed. Land

of Respirators pearling the hours,
haven of coquina ranch-styles where Venus
Fly Traps feast beneath a thriving acid-sun.

Jenniver's gone from here, but she may be
an eighteen-foot alligator hissing from
its primordial throat. If I see her again,

she may be a field of wild firewheel
intertwined with castilleja and weed.
I am the last sword sharpened by her word.

Muddy Offshoots

There's a pretty good chance she had no idea
where to find solace beyond Florida's shade,
her minuscule place amid the void.

For listless years, I went after wicked angel
dust, searched for my fathermark in every
fisherman's drunk wisdom, nursed wolf pups

beneath moonrocks—every night I'd shred
my next day's focus into smithereens.
There's a real-good chance she blew past

God's shadow, past the Hovering Gatekeepers,
past the ascendant numb people curled-in-bed
to fry her eyes beneath a glowed-up red dwarf.

In the final months, I forgot her voice,
how it bent like muddy offshoots of the Catawba,
the way she'd say *sugar* while asking for oxygen.

One of the last calls, she said,
"I hope I never see another mountain again."
Days after, the irises clamored through soil

like a perplexed crowd after Jesus broke
lit from the tomb. Why does gravity spiral
around the living? What happened

to our distant-relative Neanderthals?
When she died, I watched panthers stalk
through the Everglades shallow murk.

They lurked around a heron's nest
where the stilted quip left a half-dozen
gorging eggs. No, I was watching

Animal Planet on 4K with a box of Thin Mints.
On the longest summer weekdays, she'd cut
Tombstone pizza with scissors, smoke

Marlboros with Regis and Kelly. Tell me
to knot some yarn to a Publix bag. Go fly
a kite outside—let me think. Let me be. Get.

Levitate

Righteous future with your anti-gravity,
fearsome stairway beneath Aramaic
interstellar pinpricks whispering
as the waterwall becomes a standstill miracle.

Keep dreaming angel; nobody's going to hurt
you. Let's watch the future
freefall like a delusion of grandeur
parachuting from the stratosphere
into New Mexico like that flight suit lunatic
leaping out of his hot-air-balloon basket.
Memory works like gunk
greasing the tractor engine
before you plough the poetic field.

God's living easy now—forgetful mastermind
spilling beers and letting each continent
mop up the mess. Imagine Icarus
unshackled, weightless and finally
floating nameless as every plumed bird
before Audubon picked up a pencil.
Winged Transparent Anatomical Manikins
hover guts out and guarding a neon-blue
electric fence where the wandering dead wait
before looking for their feather-quill-written name
in a giant lambskin tome. Ghoulish schools of fin-riddled
sunfish waver above your wandered-off head
where pterodactyls sound their primordial throats
like shrill horn players and bone xylophone
drummers. Suspended mossy rocks unravel
vine veins downward and some bodies grab hold,
leave their feet to kiss the charcoal weigh-station
goodbye.

Floodwaters recede, mothers re-marry,
the devil and his angels visit the Herculean
shoulders of a different bard
because you've grown soft as summer grass
blades blown curbside in a college morass.

Harmonizing gnats whirligig like the brain
repeatedly trying to heal.

Experience Meat

Let long vowels be untouchable strings
of the Aeolian harp inside your throat.

Smooth the poem-stone with plain lingo
for the reader. Write into the meat,

your experience-meat—cut-it-up for them
to read. Make it easy, never hazy. Write

unique messages that outline what-to-do
if God just shows up one day

out of the blue. Spritz pomegranate perfume
like a little heart-throb

open in the palm of a prophet. Round
out what you say with a concept

to help a groggy man who has foggy-nothing
for a memory. Help Ralph talk to his wife

like his tongue is the first cinema opened in Alaska
and everybody's jaw drops for the camera.

Try to make movies with your words, try to carve
Mary Magdalene from scrap wood, try to run

around the neighborhood and find sublime connections
in the picked-apart bird spine. Navigate the gorgeous

circle-of-all-experience. Listen to the beat—write rhythmic
chasms from the phantom in your plasma.

Pretend the world's gone hazmat and you have to save
every idea-seed because one day it might grow

a watermelon—nobody remembers how to cut juicy
cubes, except you. Be sage with your voice. Give

as much as you can to the Hovering Guardians who keep
watch above us like the gargoyles coughing

rain off the side of Notre Dame. Save what you can
from the inevitable fires—they only want

to burn the Crown of Thorns. Keep honeypots
inside the pantry—leave your love-door ajar.

Woozy

Screwdriver-bright blinds throw day lit darts
through my iris-bullseye—two hammers start
rattling my brainpan-toolbox. Sarah plays
Apollo's lyre across the sunspot stray
hairs chording my forehead.
Her fingertips bruise the cotton
pillowcases like grenade shreds
shouting shrapnel. Bitten
teeth-marks dot my Lucky Strike
smokestack brick neck.
Behind the blinds, honeycomb patterns
octagon with camouflaged diamondbacks
laying in the bluegrass.
Sarah shakes off last night's black
flag and cracks eggs like skulls
with chocolate-chips in a metal
bowl. The Land O'Lakes girl
on the butter box kneels
inside the Land O'Lakes girl
holding a butter box—stratocumulus
migraines ripple nimbus whorls
inside my fried-control-panel
like wisteria whipping lilac shade
once a year. Deadpan knots of rhododendron
yelp near my neighbor's anxious azaleas.
Last night, I strut peacock feather-train loops
around friendly bodies and drank a whole
creek bottle dry. Now the neighbors are changing
their guitar wires on the porch, tweaking strings
until the A sharpens into halo. Somebody
blend me a tomato before I go see Mary.

All-Nighter and Vision of Ajax

"He'd fight to the death as a panther springs forth from her thicket lair," *The Iliad*

I.

After I ford Xanthous rivers in a milky haze,
a glass of tap water tastes like the mercury
broke out from a thermometer. Hayden's
shirtless, sleeping twisted in the den
on a plaid-print sofa—he's wrestling
nobody in the half-dark
like a limbless marble hunk.
The Belvedere Torso has no head;
it's been knocked-off with the most of him.
He's seated on a panther skin. Thighs thick
as mammoth gourds—is it courageous Ajax
turned coward, turning a broadsword
on himself? One fallen warrior's visage
fades into a pinprick, a shadowboxing image:
bubble-screen television blue blur—every
faucet in this hovel leaks a braid that peters
thin as Fahrenheit graduation marks.
Moonbeams divide dust on the Venetian blinds.
I go outside to watch the first blips of shy rain
fall like quarters on a velvet guitar case.
Every living person's fighting some invisible war.
Against time, against their self.
Against their body, against their health.

II.

Dawn patrol dinosaur-descendants
alarm-clock their birdsong from ancient
oaks and search the Earth for dewy grubs.
Spirits ash as bodiless dead Floridians
stagger back to hit the hay on wormy couches.
Impressionist eye-fog deceives my brain-grog
like Monet's cataracts saturating haystacks.
Wiley's calico runt of the litter
lingers in the Explorer-clogged driveway.
She's looking for tuna juice.
When Kingpin cuts a Ringo tab
from The Beatles blotter paper,
all I do is trip animals and ancient warriors
while snow leopards hunt the Himalayan
ibex as Jimi Hendrix spirals the experience
from his Stratocaster. He has this ability
to chisel the metaphorical alabaster
inside my mental quarry.

The Chiasmus Chimera

I.

In Tallahassee I started riots   put Band-Aids on broken doors   train-wrecked
     my voice box   with cigarette cartons and haircut sugar   a scissor-handed barber
with a horizon-eye for bad weather   shapes up my beard on Halloween   hair-gel hooligans
     kicked-in our front door   on Essex Drive   I was on my acid odyssey   wordsmith
with pink locks   swaggered in a double-breasted   corduroy shirt
     somebody ate my strawberry Pop-Tart   Elise was a worried sapphire
somebody caked fake-blood on vampiric cheeks   somebody was dressed as SWAT
     In Tallahassee I dressed vampiric   worried about Elise's blood   smithed strawberries
out of tart shirts   somebody said   *your skin's always pink*   I was on Essex
     driving up to our front door on Halloween   Elise had the horizon in her cigarette
after swatting at a wasp nest   my voice box needed to be opened   with scissors
     paper   with my neighbor's sugar   wolves were selling us bad weather   I was Odysseus
waking up rock-wrecked   rioting on an island of barbaric giants   In Tallahassee

II.

quitting will bring back the writhing   snakeskin   inside your brain
my father's face was sandpaper   fallen from a workbench   to be with dust
the Renegade bus   blew down Jackson Bluff   the Tomahawk bus   blew down Pensacola
my turtle-headed fellow fools   scrape mirrors   like Peter Paul Rubens paints Venus
curvy   nights at the Butter Factory   we ramped scooters over lawn chairs   launched
Barbie Jeeps over ditch creeks   threw bottle rockets in yard fires   we shaved our heads
on Blackburn and Day   we were amphibious lunatics   fueled by diner hash
Seminole church   and flaming spears   fallen from Renegade   our appaloosa savior
my father blew down his brain   and quit work to be with dust   we lit day fires
when Leo died   we held a vigil in the church lot   he went to Pensacola and flipped his Jeep
off a bridge in broad daylight   they found the truck near loggerhead turtle nesting grounds
they'll crack the sand   when June ends   every year we drive back to that bluff
near the Gulf of Mexico   we lay a wreath and fish off Leo's bridge   until we know
we need to shave   God knows   *we need to quit*

Atlantic Beach Shallows

One afternoon outside Singleton's seafood,
Kelly said, "I'm not going to sit here and blindly
connect the sky." Why the hell on earth not!

What little time we have on this dime-sized
blip of kush and fish—Christ—I'm all-about
mis-communicating everything I've misinterpreted.

Times I believed the shrimp would hum my blood-
name to call me home while the Coast Guard
searched the Atlantic Beach shallows

with spotlights for cocaine packages
floated-off from a sunken Cuban speedboat.
It's true: I am the spitting image of my fathermark,

his wayward firstborn son, walking across
the Matthew's Bridge over the Saint John's
River on my way to see a Jaguar's loss.

Why would fate divine the majority of my flea-
sized attention-span to a failed football franchise?
To the next tropical storm surf or a field in Tennessee?

More than ever, I want to radiate positivity
all-the-way past the thermosphere so
the cosmonauts can see me monkey around.

I've witnessed a fresh-from-slumber muzzled-leopard
waltz into a showroom on a leash
afore the schoolchild roars.

Sedated Apex-predator of the ancient
world, did you know your mother's yowl
from every other river sound? Where will
you roam, uncaged in the wilderness of heck?

When I was an impressionable minion,
a model for Hieronymus Bosch's demons
dancing in my triptych-brainpan, I snuck

into the Jacksonville Zoo's big cat habitat
and found a warm place to snug
where no one could say I was stranger
than every toothy beast around me.

Shade

We hung lily wreaths on the preacher's Chrysler.
Harsh shine was sweating the bricklayers.
Every steer farmer worth a fat duck's
egg in Lake City dressed in black.

All the veiled wives fanning funeral
pamphlets, your black-and-white
print face shooing horseflies—who
do you set down to dinner with now?

Keeping your Pete Rose baseball card.
Carpenter built your coffin in two days.
carved it from birch. When I got to the pond,
you were facedown in still water.

Thought you were playing around,
looking for lures or screaming at minnows.
When I pulled you out of that dead
water, an azalea stuck to your face.

We didn't need six pallbearers;
I could have lifted you myself.
Today, we put you in a Cadillac
and drove around downtown, twice.

Remember when we shared a room?
You smacked my head into the bedpost
and knocked my tooth out. Last night,
we all set down for dinner.

Chicken pot pie. I led the prayer.
First, you walk. Meet God in the glade.
When you get hot, lay in the shade.

Primordial Soup

Every night I dug a grave, followed Polaris,
speechless and wary through an all-knowing
wood. The moss-whiskered Oaks hummed,
roots engorged with sweetwater. Entire blazing
days slipped past the fingertip counting method
I had perfected. Sweat fell off my ribcage
like springtide rain on the corn. Every night, I dug
myself out from the dirt, followed stars Northward
as God's heartbeat thumped in the forest. It pulsed in hidden
creekwater murk—I drank enough to drown a draft horse.
Speechless, dark, all-knowing North nights led me through
thorns—my blood fell soft as warm rain on the cornfields.
Every night was guesswork, directionless wandering
under Polaris singing for nobody or God.
Entire galaxies burned-out while I dug a grave
to hide my body from the horsemen
hunting after my muddy feet. To think: Noah
hammered Gopherwood boards without much light.
He ignored a world of doubt to build
a floating safehouse for every voiceless beast.

Humanity is obsessed with creating
impossible structures, arranging stained glass
against the Eastern horizon, proving that Earth is both
Womb and tomb for uncountable seed, innumerable
bodies—Jean-Marc Fournier ran inside the smoking
doors of Notre Dame to save the Crown of Thorns
from turning ash when the Gothic cathedral caught fire
six days before Easter. My first night back in Florida,
I whisked a roux dark brown, mixed-in the holy trinity,
a touch more flour and let it simmer while my brother
finger-picked his acoustic guitar on the patio,
beneath a jasmine-swallowed gazebo.

The celery and carrots, the onion turned translucent,
released that intoxicating primal scent like a boar's
head screeching in silence above the lightless
dive bar's pockmarked dartboard bullseye.
The sweat that pours just hours before the preacher
clears his throat, wavering at the too-bright pulpit.

Whatever Cajun magic works her invisible power
inside this gumbo pot, I love her
Creole infinitude—I stack the outdoor logs
pyramidal for the pit.

Let the ghost peppers
give you a few hot tears
because food is religion and flavor is spirit.
My father whisks the roux while a blue flame
lives reflected in his round eyeglasses. To me,
he is wilding up a primordial soup
until it is the perfect color.

The Neanderthal Tongue

I.

I am the pterodactyl of parataxis
Hippolytus said 'the life of humankind is complete
misery' Gorgias made a fist—in Tallahassee

I tripped highlighter shoes and laced shake
like a nasty crossover
quaking ankles on a blacktop

whole cases of cheap yeast we drank
barley barrels and barely ate
when the Gulf hurricane swang rain

Got a bloody nose wrestling Leo in his muddy yard
we let the chickens run off
they couldn't have gotten far

II.

fabricating Leon County grammar
while Scout Finch bobbles in a ham costume

pigeons duck viridian domes
underneath my fingernails after work

jumping dead Neons then a Pontiac
half-mile past the Lil Champ with cherry

slurpees and hot peanuts in a crackpot
I know only the Neanderthal tongue

III.

towing broke-down Corollas then an Aztek
while Scout Finch ducks under a ham

tweaking Maycomb in a crackpot book
I only know Neanderthals and tongue

hot peanuts in a lot half-mile past the Lil Champ
blazing a bubbler of vermillion-purp with Leo

after work we chew on grammar
in a county where no one lifts a fingernail

IV.

high-stepping puddles in his spartan raincoat
Zay toe-taps Pegasus shoelaces
while his halo lungs thrust cloud nothings

a sun-void week of anguish
the frown-dappled shiver-people putter
parasols through a cold front miracle

minimalist pedestrians and hooded wanderers
quake in black jackets headed for church
bells and horsemen gallop behind the infinite

windows every thumb filing opus complaints
Nike regrets her face and humorless messengers
finalize the Dada movement by hurling apples

over Duchamp's urinal and opening their vanity
consider this hermetic yowl poetic étouffée

Guillotine

Manic shirtless neck in stocks,
you know the feeling of being loaded
headfirst, locked halfway through a box.

Now face the once-pleasant public who voted
you take the stage—the machine blade glints.
Your pulse begins splitting before a hundred

tweaked eyes. Familiar thirsty expressions
hunt across their gaunt cheekbones.
Soon, you'll join legions of legless

aimless vagrants. Your new mass: the cursed
who wander wormy intestinal mazes, termite
dugouts through whaleshark ribcages.

Forever shaken from a heart,
you'll float without roots as redwoods
shrink beneath your view. Goodbye

laughter! They want to see your face
turned gash—they want to hear your final yodel.
Roars for a few seconds. You know the image:

All those faces blending with nothing
above the sky—then a blade. Night,
then light. Light, again. Again.

How to Create a Boy Out of Thunder

Pull an arrowhead from the riverbed.
Turn the spearpoint over in your hand.
Cup your palms around a minnow

in the shallows. A drop of blood
catching numb light—his portrait
poised on the edge of buck knife.

Cut his tongue out. In its place, stitch
a stingray's barb. Cut him a centerpiece
of chocolate cake. Table his slice

until the floured eggs and coconut
flake into a baked plate of ash.
Pick up a spent bullet shell

near the driveway anthill. Pour
a gallon of gasoline in the mound.
Drop a match—a writhing hive of fire.

Lacewings buzz infinity against
perpetual azaleas. Shade a grid of leaves
with charcoal dusk. Shed the world's husk

and fly to hell with him. Light cherry
bomb fuses, then toss exploding roses
as bottle rocket sparks spin Pepsi

lips on a blacktop—the only proof
he was ever even here.

Beyond the Garden

I.

Disarm the chubby, holy sword-wielding
son sent down—set his baby hair on fire.
Do it before he splits-open this edenic

lush. Whisper every name
under the falling cinders.

Scratch wordsymbols on sandbanks—hightail-it
up loose dune sand and bleed in a shallow creek.

II.

Stream between billion-year-old limestone
slabs—dance the colors on a bunting's wing.

Primordial shriek a world
out of the ibis' throat—make blue
herons poke wild shrimp

ghosting through the brackish
haven. Embody the Neanderthal

and carve a piece of alabaster—
articulate her triangular hips.

III.

Kneel beneath an indifferent scattershot
of omniscient far light.

Ring buoy bells
beyond waking waves—be a pink streak
erasing the horizon and make every edge

curvaceous. Roar a waterfall ledge—weave
sweetgrass into Earth's fishtail braid.

IV.

Reek mushrooms out of deer scat,
     gather each fallen leaf, then lay a wreath
before your creator's cavern tomb. Tap sap
from maples—drink the unfamiliar drip
     straight off the sweet bark.

As the Den Burns

It was about to close, no matter what.
No matter what we said, it was going to close.
Everything was shutting down, closing up.
Ending time was drawing closer. We swore
we wouldn't ever do it again—no matter
what. The light was going down. We swore
it was an accident, an experiment, a one
time thing. We did it for the experience;
we didn't know better. No matter what
we said, we looked guilty. Dirtier, somehow.
Every plant was closing and shutting.
Light was going down on every piece
of the world. Unfamiliar silence
made us frantic. It was going to close
no matter what. Then, everything
started getting brighter. Our shame
began to fade with the old world we knew
and loved. Our bodies started looking better
than ever, so we wanted to do it again and again.
This is how the old world ended.
It closed up, shut down into zero light.
A period of silence. We knew too much
about the origin of everything, as if
our bodies molded-together
once held the original light
and we were just an experiment.
A one time thing.
Guilty as the shameless dirt
where we stood, trembling.
The original light began to vanish.
It stopped illuminating the dust
on our bodies—we were blown out.
Waved out. Then we heard the twin-doors shut.
Fires began burning on the old wall as it shut
tight behind us. We were swearing in a primal,
loveless way. We lost all communication.
Our tongues fell numb. Without language
or the ability to plea, we grew frantic
as the light went down, then every piece of the place
we knew and loved went up in flames—we did it once.

Acknowledgments

Thank you to the following journals for their belief in this poetry.

Best New Poets, "One Thousand Tongues"
PeatSmoke, "Millennia of Heck"
Waccamaw, "Fathermark"
Borderlands: Texas Poetry Review, "Radio Pop"
Windhover, "Burial," "Godchild"
Prime Number, "Disturbed Mud"
Chattahoochee Review, "Curse"
The Boiler, "Panther"
Asheville Poetry Review, "Lackawanna Crib," "Fatherbeast"
Rabid Oak, "Atlantic Baptism"
Tiger Moth Review, "From Jupiter"
Appalachian Review, "Rowing Out of a Riptide"
Greensboro Review, "Appaloosa Rider Unchained"
Santa Clara Review, "Beneath the Lemon Tree," "Firewheel"
Cold Mountain Review, "Experience Meat"
Plath Poetry Project, "Woozy"
Wraparound South, "Atlantic Beach Shallows"
Saw Palm, "Shade"
Shift, "Primordial Soup"
Miracle Monocle, "The Neanderthal Tongue"

The epigraph for part one quotes a line from Frank Stanford's epic *The Battlefield Where The Moon Says I Love You* (Lost Roads Publishing, 2000).

The epigraph for part two quotes a line from Homer's epic *The Odyssey* translated by Robert Fitzgerald (Vintage Classics, 1990).

The epigraph for part three quotes a line from William Faulkner's novel *The Sound and the Fury* (Vintage International, 1990).

"All-Nighter and Vision of Ajax" contains an epigraph from *The Iliad* translated by Robert Fagles (Penguin Classics, 1990).

"Firewheel" and "Muddy Offshoots" were written for Jenniver Holton (1943-2019).

About the Author

Forrest Rapier has appeared in *Asheville Poetry Review, Best New Poets, Cold Mountain Review, Levee,* and *Rabid Oak,* among many others. He has received fellowships from Looking Glass Falls, Sewanee Writers Conference, and has held writing residencies at the University of Virginia and Brevard College. He received his MFA from the University of North Carolina at Greensboro where he now lives and hikes the surrounding Blue Ridge Mountains.